MW01296600

THIS NOTEBOOK BELONGS TO:

_____

Synchro Notebooks

A

WEBSITE:	
USERNAME:	
PASSWORD:	
NOTES:	

WEBSITE:	
USERNAME:	
PASSWORD:	
NOTES:	

WEBSITE:	
USERNAME:	
PASSWORD:	
NOTES:	

WEBSITE:	
USERNAME:	
PASSWORD:	
NOTES:	

WEBSITE:
USERNAME:
PASSWORD:
NOTES:

WEBSITE:
USERNAME:
PASSWORD:
NOTES:

WEBSITE:
USERNAME:
PASSWORD:
NOTES:

WEBSITE:
USERNAME:
PASSWORD:
NOTES:

A

WEBSITE:
USERNAME:
PASSWORD:
NOTES:

WEBSITE:
USERNAME:
PASSWORD:
NOTES:

WEBSITE:
USERNAME:
PASSWORD:
NOTES:

WEBSITE:
USERNAME:
PASSWORD:
NOTES:

WEBSITE:
USERNAME:
PASSWORD:
NOTES:

WEBSITE:
USERNAME:
PASSWORD:
NOTES:

WEBSITE:
USERNAME:
PASSWORD:
NOTES:

WEBSITE:
USERNAME:
PASSWORD:
NOTES:

B

WEBSITE:
USERNAME:
PASSWORD:
NOTES:

WEBSITE:
USERNAME:
PASSWORD:
NOTES:

WEBSITE:
USERNAME:
PASSWORD:
NOTES:

WEBSITE:
USERNAME:
PASSWORD:
NOTES:

B

WEBSITE:
USERNAME:
PASSWORD:
NOTES:

WEBSITE:
USERNAME:
PASSWORD:
NOTES:

WEBSITE:
USERNAME:
PASSWORD:
NOTES:

WEBSITE:
USERNAME:
PASSWORD:
NOTES:

WEBSITE:	
USERNAME:	
PASSWORD:	
NOTES:	

WEBSITE:	
USERNAME:	
PASSWORD:	
NOTES:	

WEBSITE:	
USERNAME:	
PASSWORD:	
NOTES:	

WEBSITE:	
USERNAME:	
PASSWORD:	
NOTES:	

WEBSITE:
USERNAME:
PASSWORD:
NOTES:

WEBSITE:
USERNAME:
PASSWORD:
NOTES:

WEBSITE:
USERNAME:
PASSWORD:
NOTES:

WEBSITE:
USERNAME:
PASSWORD:
NOTES:

| WEBSITE: |
| USERNAME: |
| PASSWORD: |
| NOTES: |
| |
| |

| WEBSITE: |
| USERNAME: |
| PASSWORD: |
| NOTES: |
| |
| |

| WEBSITE: |
| USERNAME: |
| PASSWORD: |
| NOTES: |
| |
| |

| WEBSITE: |
| USERNAME: |
| PASSWORD: |
| NOTES: |
| |
| |

WEBSITE:	
USERNAME:	
PASSWORD:	
NOTES:	

WEBSITE:	
USERNAME:	
PASSWORD:	
NOTES:	

WEBSITE:	
USERNAME:	
PASSWORD:	
NOTES:	

WEBSITE:	
USERNAME:	
PASSWORD:	
NOTES:	

C

WEBSITE:	
USERNAME:	
PASSWORD:	
NOTES:	

WEBSITE:	
USERNAME:	
PASSWORD:	
NOTES:	

WEBSITE:	
USERNAME:	
PASSWORD:	
NOTES:	

WEBSITE:	
USERNAME:	
PASSWORD:	
NOTES:	

C

| WEBSITE: |
| USERNAME: |
| PASSWORD: |
| NOTES: |
| |
| |

| WEBSITE: |
| USERNAME: |
| PASSWORD: |
| NOTES: |
| |
| |

| WEBSITE: |
| USERNAME: |
| PASSWORD: |
| NOTES: |
| |
| |

| WEBSITE: |
| USERNAME: |
| PASSWORD: |
| NOTES: |
| |
| |

D

WEBSITE:
USERNAME:
PASSWORD:
NOTES:

WEBSITE:
USERNAME:
PASSWORD:
NOTES:

WEBSITE:
USERNAME:
PASSWORD:
NOTES:

WEBSITE:
USERNAME:
PASSWORD:
NOTES:

WEBSITE:
USERNAME:
PASSWORD:
NOTES:

WEBSITE:
USERNAME:
PASSWORD:
NOTES:

WEBSITE:
USERNAME:
PASSWORD:
NOTES:

WEBSITE:
USERNAME:
PASSWORD:
NOTES:

D

WEBSITE:
USERNAME:
PASSWORD:
NOTES:

WEBSITE:
USERNAME:
PASSWORD:
NOTES:

WEBSITE:
USERNAME:
PASSWORD:
NOTES:

WEBSITE:
USERNAME:
PASSWORD:
NOTES:

D

WEBSITE:
USERNAME:
PASSWORD:
NOTES:

WEBSITE:
USERNAME:
PASSWORD:
NOTES:

WEBSITE:
USERNAME:
PASSWORD:
NOTES:

WEBSITE:
USERNAME:
PASSWORD:
NOTES:

E

WEBSITE:
USERNAME:
PASSWORD:
NOTES:

WEBSITE:
USERNAME:
PASSWORD:
NOTES:

WEBSITE:
USERNAME:
PASSWORD:
NOTES:

WEBSITE:
USERNAME:
PASSWORD:
NOTES:

| WEBSITE: |
| USERNAME: |
| PASSWORD: |
| NOTES: |
| |
| |

| WEBSITE: |
| USERNAME: |
| PASSWORD: |
| NOTES: |
| |
| |

| WEBSITE: |
| USERNAME: |
| PASSWORD: |
| NOTES: |
| |
| |

| WEBSITE: |
| USERNAME: |
| PASSWORD: |
| NOTES: |
| |
| |

WEBSITE:
USERNAME:
PASSWORD:
NOTES:

WEBSITE:
USERNAME:
PASSWORD:
NOTES:

WEBSITE:
USERNAME:
PASSWORD:
NOTES:

WEBSITE:
USERNAME:
PASSWORD:
NOTES:

WEBSITE:

USERNAME:

PASSWORD:

NOTES:

WEBSITE:

USERNAME:

PASSWORD:

NOTES:

WEBSITE:

USERNAME:

PASSWORD:

NOTES:

WEBSITE:

USERNAME:

PASSWORD:

NOTES:

WEBSITE:
USERNAME:
PASSWORD:
NOTES:

WEBSITE:
USERNAME:
PASSWORD:
NOTES:

WEBSITE:
USERNAME:
PASSWORD:
NOTES:

WEBSITE:
USERNAME:
PASSWORD:
NOTES:

F

WEBSITE:
USERNAME:
PASSWORD:
NOTES:

WEBSITE:
USERNAME:
PASSWORD:
NOTES:

WEBSITE:
USERNAME:
PASSWORD:
NOTES:

WEBSITE:
USERNAME:
PASSWORD:
NOTES:

WEBSITE:

USERNAME:

PASSWORD:

NOTES:

WEBSITE:

USERNAME:

PASSWORD:

NOTES:

WEBSITE:

USERNAME:

PASSWORD:

NOTES:

WEBSITE:

USERNAME:

PASSWORD:

NOTES:

| WEBSITE: |
| USERNAME: |
| PASSWORD: |
| NOTES: |
| |
| |

| WEBSITE: |
| USERNAME: |
| PASSWORD: |
| NOTES: |
| |
| |

| WEBSITE: |
| USERNAME: |
| PASSWORD: |
| NOTES: |
| |
| |

| WEBSITE: |
| USERNAME: |
| PASSWORD: |
| NOTES: |
| |
| |

G

WEBSITE:
USERNAME:
PASSWORD:
NOTES:

WEBSITE:
USERNAME:
PASSWORD:
NOTES:

WEBSITE:
USERNAME:
PASSWORD:
NOTES:

WEBSITE:
USERNAME:
PASSWORD:
NOTES:

G

| WEBSITE: |
| USERNAME: |
| PASSWORD: |
| NOTES: |
| |
| |

| WEBSITE: |
| USERNAME: |
| PASSWORD: |
| NOTES: |
| |
| |

| WEBSITE: |
| USERNAME: |
| PASSWORD: |
| NOTES: |
| |
| |

| WEBSITE: |
| USERNAME: |
| PASSWORD: |
| NOTES: |
| |
| |

G

WEBSITE:
USERNAME:
PASSWORD:
NOTES:

WEBSITE:
USERNAME:
PASSWORD:
NOTES:

WEBSITE:
USERNAME:
PASSWORD:
NOTES:

WEBSITE:
USERNAME:
PASSWORD:
NOTES:

G

WEBSITE:
USERNAME:
PASSWORD:
NOTES:

WEBSITE:
USERNAME:
PASSWORD:
NOTES:

WEBSITE:
USERNAME:
PASSWORD:
NOTES:

WEBSITE:
USERNAME:
PASSWORD:
NOTES:

WEBSITE:

USERNAME:

PASSWORD:

NOTES:

WEBSITE:

USERNAME:

PASSWORD:

NOTES:

WEBSITE:

USERNAME:

PASSWORD:

NOTES:

WEBSITE:

USERNAME:

PASSWORD:

NOTES:

| WEBSITE: |
| USERNAME: |
| PASSWORD: |
| NOTES: |
| |
| |

| WEBSITE: |
| USERNAME: |
| PASSWORD: |
| NOTES: |
| |
| |

| WEBSITE: |
| USERNAME: |
| PASSWORD: |
| NOTES: |
| |
| |

| WEBSITE: |
| USERNAME: |
| PASSWORD: |
| NOTES: |
| |
| |

WEBSITE:	
USERNAME:	
PASSWORD:	
NOTES:	

WEBSITE:	
USERNAME:	
PASSWORD:	
NOTES:	

WEBSITE:	
USERNAME:	
PASSWORD:	
NOTES:	

WEBSITE:	
USERNAME:	
PASSWORD:	
NOTES:	

| WEBSITE: |
| USERNAME: |
| PASSWORD: |
| NOTES: |
| |
| |

| WEBSITE: |
| USERNAME: |
| PASSWORD: |
| NOTES: |
| |
| |

| WEBSITE: |
| USERNAME: |
| PASSWORD: |
| NOTES: |
| |
| |

| WEBSITE: |
| USERNAME: |
| PASSWORD: |
| NOTES: |
| |
| |

WEBSITE:
USERNAME:
PASSWORD:
NOTES:

WEBSITE:
USERNAME:
PASSWORD:
NOTES:

WEBSITE:
USERNAME:
PASSWORD:
NOTES:

WEBSITE:
USERNAME:
PASSWORD:
NOTES:

WEBSITE:
USERNAME:
PASSWORD:
NOTES:

WEBSITE:
USERNAME:
PASSWORD:
NOTES:

WEBSITE:
USERNAME:
PASSWORD:
NOTES:

WEBSITE:
USERNAME:
PASSWORD:
NOTES:

WEBSITE:

USERNAME:

PASSWORD:

NOTES:

WEBSITE:

USERNAME:

PASSWORD:

NOTES:

WEBSITE:

USERNAME:

PASSWORD:

NOTES:

WEBSITE:

USERNAME:

PASSWORD:

NOTES:

WEBSITE:
USERNAME:
PASSWORD:
NOTES:

WEBSITE:
USERNAME:
PASSWORD:
NOTES:

WEBSITE:
USERNAME:
PASSWORD:
NOTES:

WEBSITE:
USERNAME:
PASSWORD:
NOTES:

J

WEBSITE:

USERNAME:

PASSWORD:

NOTES:

WEBSITE:

USERNAME:

PASSWORD:

NOTES:

WEBSITE:

USERNAME:

PASSWORD:

NOTES:

WEBSITE:

USERNAME:

PASSWORD:

NOTES:

WEBSITE:

USERNAME:

PASSWORD:

NOTES:

WEBSITE:

USERNAME:

PASSWORD:

NOTES:

WEBSITE:

USERNAME:

PASSWORD:

NOTES:

WEBSITE:

USERNAME:

PASSWORD:

NOTES:

J

WEBSITE:
USERNAME:
PASSWORD:
NOTES:

WEBSITE:
USERNAME:
PASSWORD:
NOTES:

WEBSITE:
USERNAME:
PASSWORD:
NOTES:

WEBSITE:
USERNAME:
PASSWORD:
NOTES:

| **WEBSITE:** |
| **USERNAME:** |
| **PASSWORD:** |
| **NOTES:** |
| |
| |

| **WEBSITE:** |
| **USERNAME:** |
| **PASSWORD:** |
| **NOTES:** |
| |
| |

| **WEBSITE:** |
| **USERNAME:** |
| **PASSWORD:** |
| **NOTES:** |
| |
| |

| **WEBSITE:** |
| **USERNAME:** |
| **PASSWORD:** |
| **NOTES:** |
| |
| |

K

WEBSITE:	
USERNAME:	
PASSWORD:	
NOTES:	

WEBSITE:	
USERNAME:	
PASSWORD:	
NOTES:	

WEBSITE:	
USERNAME:	
PASSWORD:	
NOTES:	

WEBSITE:	
USERNAME:	
PASSWORD:	
NOTES:	

WEBSITE:

USERNAME:

PASSWORD:

NOTES:

WEBSITE:

USERNAME:

PASSWORD:

NOTES:

WEBSITE:

USERNAME:

PASSWORD:

NOTES:

WEBSITE:

USERNAME:

PASSWORD:

NOTES:

K

WEBSITE:
USERNAME:
PASSWORD:
NOTES:

WEBSITE:
USERNAME:
PASSWORD:
NOTES:

WEBSITE:
USERNAME:
PASSWORD:
NOTES:

WEBSITE:
USERNAME:
PASSWORD:
NOTES:

WEBSITE:

USERNAME:

PASSWORD:

NOTES:

WEBSITE:

USERNAME:

PASSWORD:

NOTES:

WEBSITE:

USERNAME:

PASSWORD:

NOTES:

WEBSITE:

USERNAME:

PASSWORD:

NOTES:

WEBSITE:
USERNAME:
PASSWORD:
NOTES:

WEBSITE:
USERNAME:
PASSWORD:
NOTES:

WEBSITE:
USERNAME:
PASSWORD:
NOTES:

WEBSITE:
USERNAME:
PASSWORD:
NOTES:

WEBSITE:
USERNAME:
PASSWORD:
NOTES:

WEBSITE:
USERNAME:
PASSWORD:
NOTES:

WEBSITE:
USERNAME:
PASSWORD:
NOTES:

WEBSITE:
USERNAME:
PASSWORD:
NOTES:

L

WEBSITE:
USERNAME:
PASSWORD:
NOTES:

WEBSITE:
USERNAME:
PASSWORD:
NOTES:

WEBSITE:
USERNAME:
PASSWORD:
NOTES:

WEBSITE:
USERNAME:
PASSWORD:
NOTES:

WEBSITE:

USERNAME:

PASSWORD:

NOTES:

WEBSITE:

USERNAME:

PASSWORD:

NOTES:

WEBSITE:

USERNAME:

PASSWORD:

NOTES:

WEBSITE:

USERNAME:

PASSWORD:

NOTES:

WEBSITE:
USERNAME:
PASSWORD:
NOTES:

WEBSITE:
USERNAME:
PASSWORD:
NOTES:

WEBSITE:
USERNAME:
PASSWORD:
NOTES:

WEBSITE:
USERNAME:
PASSWORD:
NOTES:

WEBSITE:

USERNAME:

PASSWORD:

NOTES:

WEBSITE:

USERNAME:

PASSWORD:

NOTES:

WEBSITE:

USERNAME:

PASSWORD:

NOTES:

WEBSITE:

USERNAME:

PASSWORD:

NOTES:

WEBSITE:
USERNAME:
PASSWORD:
NOTES:

WEBSITE:
USERNAME:
PASSWORD:
NOTES:

WEBSITE:
USERNAME:
PASSWORD:
NOTES:

WEBSITE:
USERNAME:
PASSWORD:
NOTES:

WEBSITE:

USERNAME:

PASSWORD:

NOTES:

WEBSITE:

USERNAME:

PASSWORD:

NOTES:

WEBSITE:

USERNAME:

PASSWORD:

NOTES:

WEBSITE:

USERNAME:

PASSWORD:

NOTES:

WEBSITE:
USERNAME:
PASSWORD:
NOTES:

WEBSITE:
USERNAME:
PASSWORD:
NOTES:

WEBSITE:
USERNAME:
PASSWORD:
NOTES:

WEBSITE:
USERNAME:
PASSWORD:
NOTES:

WEBSITE:

USERNAME:

PASSWORD:

NOTES:

WEBSITE:

USERNAME:

PASSWORD:

NOTES:

WEBSITE:

USERNAME:

PASSWORD:

NOTES:

WEBSITE:

USERNAME:

PASSWORD:

NOTES:

WEBSITE:	
USERNAME:	
PASSWORD:	
NOTES:	

WEBSITE:	
USERNAME:	
PASSWORD:	
NOTES:	

WEBSITE:	
USERNAME:	
PASSWORD:	
NOTES:	

WEBSITE:	
USERNAME:	
PASSWORD:	
NOTES:	

WEBSITE:

USERNAME:

PASSWORD:

NOTES:

WEBSITE:

USERNAME:

PASSWORD:

NOTES:

WEBSITE:

USERNAME:

PASSWORD:

NOTES:

WEBSITE:

USERNAME:

PASSWORD:

NOTES:

WEBSITE:
USERNAME:
PASSWORD:
NOTES:

WEBSITE:
USERNAME:
PASSWORD:
NOTES:

WEBSITE:
USERNAME:
PASSWORD:
NOTES:

WEBSITE:
USERNAME:
PASSWORD:
NOTES:

| WEBSITE: |
| USERNAME: |
| PASSWORD: |
| NOTES: |
| |
| |

| WEBSITE: |
| USERNAME: |
| PASSWORD: |
| NOTES: |
| |
| |

| WEBSITE: |
| USERNAME: |
| PASSWORD: |
| NOTES: |
| |
| |

| WEBSITE: |
| USERNAME: |
| PASSWORD: |
| NOTES: |
| |
| |

WEBSITE:
USERNAME:
PASSWORD:
NOTES:

WEBSITE:
USERNAME:
PASSWORD:
NOTES:

WEBSITE:
USERNAME:
PASSWORD:
NOTES:

WEBSITE:
USERNAME:
PASSWORD:
NOTES:

WEBSITE:
USERNAME:
PASSWORD:
NOTES:

WEBSITE:
USERNAME:
PASSWORD:
NOTES:

WEBSITE:
USERNAME:
PASSWORD:
NOTES:

WEBSITE:
USERNAME:
PASSWORD:
NOTES:

WEBSITE:
USERNAME:
PASSWORD:
NOTES:

WEBSITE:
USERNAME:
PASSWORD:
NOTES:

WEBSITE:
USERNAME:
PASSWORD:
NOTES:

WEBSITE:
USERNAME:
PASSWORD:
NOTES:

WEBSITE:

USERNAME:

PASSWORD:

NOTES:

WEBSITE:

USERNAME:

PASSWORD:

NOTES:

WEBSITE:

USERNAME:

PASSWORD:

NOTES:

WEBSITE:

USERNAME:

PASSWORD:

NOTES:

WEBSITE:
USERNAME:
PASSWORD:
NOTES:

WEBSITE:
USERNAME:
PASSWORD:
NOTES:

WEBSITE:
USERNAME:
PASSWORD:
NOTES:

WEBSITE:
USERNAME:
PASSWORD:
NOTES:

WEBSITE:
USERNAME:
PASSWORD:
NOTES:

WEBSITE:
USERNAME:
PASSWORD:
NOTES:

WEBSITE:
USERNAME:
PASSWORD:
NOTES:

WEBSITE:
USERNAME:
PASSWORD:
NOTES:

| **WEBSITE:** |
| **USERNAME:** |
| **PASSWORD:** |
| **NOTES:** |
| |
| |

| **WEBSITE:** |
| **USERNAME:** |
| **PASSWORD:** |
| **NOTES:** |
| |
| |

| **WEBSITE:** |
| **USERNAME:** |
| **PASSWORD:** |
| **NOTES:** |
| |
| |

| **WEBSITE:** |
| **USERNAME:** |
| **PASSWORD:** |
| **NOTES:** |
| |
| |

WEBSITE:

USERNAME:

PASSWORD:

NOTES:

WEBSITE:

USERNAME:

PASSWORD:

NOTES:

WEBSITE:

USERNAME:

PASSWORD:

NOTES:

WEBSITE:

USERNAME:

PASSWORD:

NOTES:

Q

WEBSITE:
USERNAME:
PASSWORD:
NOTES:

WEBSITE:
USERNAME:
PASSWORD:
NOTES:

WEBSITE:
USERNAME:
PASSWORD:
NOTES:

WEBSITE:
USERNAME:
PASSWORD:
NOTES:

WEBSITE:
USERNAME:
PASSWORD:
NOTES:

WEBSITE:
USERNAME:
PASSWORD:
NOTES:

WEBSITE:
USERNAME:
PASSWORD:
NOTES:

WEBSITE:
USERNAME:
PASSWORD:
NOTES:

WEBSITE:

USERNAME:

PASSWORD:

NOTES:

WEBSITE:

USERNAME:

PASSWORD:

NOTES:

WEBSITE:

USERNAME:

PASSWORD:

NOTES:

WEBSITE:

USERNAME:

PASSWORD:

NOTES:

WEBSITE:
USERNAME:
PASSWORD:
NOTES:

WEBSITE:
USERNAME:
PASSWORD:
NOTES:

WEBSITE:
USERNAME:
PASSWORD:
NOTES:

WEBSITE:
USERNAME:
PASSWORD:
NOTES:

WEBSITE:
USERNAME:
PASSWORD:
NOTES:

WEBSITE:
USERNAME:
PASSWORD:
NOTES:

WEBSITE:
USERNAME:
PASSWORD:
NOTES:

WEBSITE:
USERNAME:
PASSWORD:
NOTES:

WEBSITE:
USERNAME:
PASSWORD:
NOTES:

WEBSITE:
USERNAME:
PASSWORD:
NOTES:

WEBSITE:
USERNAME:
PASSWORD:
NOTES:

WEBSITE:
USERNAME:
PASSWORD:
NOTES:

WEBSITE:	
USERNAME:	
PASSWORD:	
NOTES:	

WEBSITE:	
USERNAME:	
PASSWORD:	
NOTES:	

WEBSITE:	
USERNAME:	
PASSWORD:	
NOTES:	

WEBSITE:	
USERNAME:	
PASSWORD:	
NOTES:	

S

| WEBSITE: |
| USERNAME: |
| PASSWORD: |
| NOTES: |
| |
| |

| WEBSITE: |
| USERNAME: |
| PASSWORD: |
| NOTES: |
| |
| |

| WEBSITE: |
| USERNAME: |
| PASSWORD: |
| NOTES: |
| |
| |

| WEBSITE: |
| USERNAME: |
| PASSWORD: |
| NOTES: |
| |
| |

WEBSITE:
USERNAME:
PASSWORD:
NOTES:

WEBSITE:
USERNAME:
PASSWORD:
NOTES:

WEBSITE:
USERNAME:
PASSWORD:
NOTES:

WEBSITE:
USERNAME:
PASSWORD:
NOTES:

S

| WEBSITE: |
| USERNAME: |
| PASSWORD: |
| NOTES: |
| |
| |

| WEBSITE: |
| USERNAME: |
| PASSWORD: |
| NOTES: |
| |
| |

| WEBSITE: |
| USERNAME: |
| PASSWORD: |
| NOTES: |
| |
| |

| WEBSITE: |
| USERNAME: |
| PASSWORD: |
| NOTES: |
| |
| |

WEBSITE:	
USERNAME:	
PASSWORD:	
NOTES:	

WEBSITE:	
USERNAME:	
PASSWORD:	
NOTES:	

WEBSITE:	
USERNAME:	
PASSWORD:	
NOTES:	

WEBSITE:	
USERNAME:	
PASSWORD:	
NOTES:	

WEBSITE:

USERNAME:

PASSWORD:

NOTES:

WEBSITE:

USERNAME:

PASSWORD:

NOTES:

WEBSITE:

USERNAME:

PASSWORD:

NOTES:

WEBSITE:

USERNAME:

PASSWORD:

NOTES:

WEBSITE:	
USERNAME:	
PASSWORD:	
NOTES:	

WEBSITE:	
USERNAME:	
PASSWORD:	
NOTES:	

WEBSITE:	
USERNAME:	
PASSWORD:	
NOTES:	

WEBSITE:	
USERNAME:	
PASSWORD:	
NOTES:	

| WEBSITE: |
| USERNAME: |
| PASSWORD: |
| NOTES: |
| |
| |

| WEBSITE: |
| USERNAME: |
| PASSWORD: |
| NOTES: |
| |
| |

| WEBSITE: |
| USERNAME: |
| PASSWORD: |
| NOTES: |
| |
| |

| WEBSITE: |
| USERNAME: |
| PASSWORD: |
| NOTES: |
| |
| |

WEBSITE:
USERNAME:
PASSWORD:
NOTES:

WEBSITE:
USERNAME:
PASSWORD:
NOTES:

WEBSITE:
USERNAME:
PASSWORD:
NOTES:

WEBSITE:
USERNAME:
PASSWORD:
NOTES:

WEBSITE:

USERNAME:

PASSWORD:

NOTES:

WEBSITE:

USERNAME:

PASSWORD:

NOTES:

WEBSITE:

USERNAME:

PASSWORD:

NOTES:

WEBSITE:

USERNAME:

PASSWORD:

NOTES:

WEBSITE:
USERNAME:
PASSWORD:
NOTES:

WEBSITE:
USERNAME:
PASSWORD:
NOTES:

WEBSITE:
USERNAME:
PASSWORD:
NOTES:

WEBSITE:
USERNAME:
PASSWORD:
NOTES:

WEBSITE:	
USERNAME:	
PASSWORD:	
NOTES:	

WEBSITE:	
USERNAME:	
PASSWORD:	
NOTES:	

WEBSITE:	
USERNAME:	
PASSWORD:	
NOTES:	

WEBSITE:	
USERNAME:	
PASSWORD:	
NOTES:	

WEBSITE:
USERNAME:
PASSWORD:
NOTES:

WEBSITE:
USERNAME:
PASSWORD:
NOTES:

WEBSITE:
USERNAME:
PASSWORD:
NOTES:

WEBSITE:
USERNAME:
PASSWORD:
NOTES:

WEBSITE:

USERNAME:

PASSWORD:

NOTES:

WEBSITE:

USERNAME:

PASSWORD:

NOTES:

WEBSITE:

USERNAME:

PASSWORD:

NOTES:

WEBSITE:

USERNAME:

PASSWORD:

NOTES:

WEBSITE:	
USERNAME:	
PASSWORD:	
NOTES:	

WEBSITE:	
USERNAME:	
PASSWORD:	
NOTES:	

WEBSITE:	
USERNAME:	
PASSWORD:	
NOTES:	

WEBSITE:	
USERNAME:	
PASSWORD:	
NOTES:	

WEBSITE:
USERNAME:
PASSWORD:
NOTES:

WEBSITE:
USERNAME:
PASSWORD:
NOTES:

WEBSITE:
USERNAME:
PASSWORD:
NOTES:

WEBSITE:
USERNAME:
PASSWORD:
NOTES:

| WEBSITE: |
| USERNAME: |
| PASSWORD: |
| NOTES: |
| |
| |
| |

| WEBSITE: |
| USERNAME: |
| PASSWORD: |
| NOTES: |
| |
| |
| |

| WEBSITE: |
| USERNAME: |
| PASSWORD: |
| NOTES: |
| |
| |
| |

| WEBSITE: |
| USERNAME: |
| PASSWORD: |
| NOTES: |
| |
| |
| |

WEBSITE:

USERNAME:

PASSWORD:

NOTES:

WEBSITE:

USERNAME:

PASSWORD:

NOTES:

WEBSITE:

USERNAME:

PASSWORD:

NOTES:

WEBSITE:

USERNAME:

PASSWORD:

NOTES:

WEBSITE:	
USERNAME:	
PASSWORD:	
NOTES:	

WEBSITE:	
USERNAME:	
PASSWORD:	
NOTES:	

WEBSITE:	
USERNAME:	
PASSWORD:	
NOTES:	

WEBSITE:	
USERNAME:	
PASSWORD:	
NOTES:	

WEBSITE:

USERNAME:

PASSWORD:

NOTES:

WEBSITE:

USERNAME:

PASSWORD:

NOTES:

WEBSITE:

USERNAME:

PASSWORD:

NOTES:

WEBSITE:

USERNAME:

PASSWORD:

NOTES:

WEBSITE:	
USERNAME:	
PASSWORD:	
NOTES:	

WEBSITE:	
USERNAME:	
PASSWORD:	
NOTES:	

WEBSITE:	
USERNAME:	
PASSWORD:	
NOTES:	

WEBSITE:	
USERNAME:	
PASSWORD:	
NOTES:	

WEBSITE:	
USERNAME:	
PASSWORD:	
NOTES:	

WEBSITE:	
USERNAME:	
PASSWORD:	
NOTES:	

WEBSITE:	
USERNAME:	
PASSWORD:	
NOTES:	

WEBSITE:	
USERNAME:	
PASSWORD:	
NOTES:	

| WEBSITE: |
| USERNAME: |
| PASSWORD: |
| NOTES: |
| |
| |

| WEBSITE: |
| USERNAME: |
| PASSWORD: |
| NOTES: |
| |
| |

| WEBSITE: |
| USERNAME: |
| PASSWORD: |
| NOTES: |
| |
| |

| WEBSITE: |
| USERNAME: |
| PASSWORD: |
| NOTES: |
| |
| |

| WEBSITE: |
| USERNAME: |
| PASSWORD: |
| NOTES: |
| |
| |

| WEBSITE: |
| USERNAME: |
| PASSWORD: |
| NOTES: |
| |
| |

| WEBSITE: |
| USERNAME: |
| PASSWORD: |
| NOTES: |
| |
| |

| WEBSITE: |
| USERNAME: |
| PASSWORD: |
| NOTES: |
| |
| |

| WEBSITE: |
| USERNAME: |
| PASSWORD: |
| NOTES: |
| |
| |

| WEBSITE: |
| USERNAME: |
| PASSWORD: |
| NOTES: |
| |
| |

| WEBSITE: |
| USERNAME: |
| PASSWORD: |
| NOTES: |
| |
| |

| WEBSITE: |
| USERNAME: |
| PASSWORD: |
| NOTES: |
| |
| |

WEBSITE:
USERNAME:
PASSWORD:
NOTES:

WEBSITE:
USERNAME:
PASSWORD:
NOTES:

WEBSITE:
USERNAME:
PASSWORD:
NOTES:

WEBSITE:
USERNAME:
PASSWORD:
NOTES:

WEBSITE:
USERNAME:
PASSWORD:
NOTES:

WEBSITE:
USERNAME:
PASSWORD:
NOTES:

WEBSITE:
USERNAME:
PASSWORD:
NOTES:

WEBSITE:
USERNAME:
PASSWORD:
NOTES:

WEBSITE:
USERNAME:
PASSWORD:
NOTES:

WEBSITE:
USERNAME:
PASSWORD:
NOTES:

WEBSITE:
USERNAME:
PASSWORD:
NOTES:

WEBSITE:
USERNAME:
PASSWORD:
NOTES:

WEBSITE:
USERNAME:
PASSWORD:
NOTES:

WEBSITE:
USERNAME:
PASSWORD:
NOTES:

WEBSITE:
USERNAME:
PASSWORD:
NOTES:

WEBSITE:
USERNAME:
PASSWORD:
NOTES:

WEBSITE:

USERNAME:

PASSWORD:

NOTES:

WEBSITE:

USERNAME:

PASSWORD:

NOTES:

WEBSITE:

USERNAME:

PASSWORD:

NOTES:

WEBSITE:

USERNAME:

PASSWORD:

NOTES:

Z

WEBSITE:	
USERNAME:	
PASSWORD:	
NOTES:	

WEBSITE:	
USERNAME:	
PASSWORD:	
NOTES:	

WEBSITE:	
USERNAME:	
PASSWORD:	
NOTES:	

WEBSITE:	
USERNAME:	
PASSWORD:	
NOTES:	

Z

WEBSITE:
USERNAME:
PASSWORD:
NOTES:

WEBSITE:
USERNAME:
PASSWORD:
NOTES:

WEBSITE:
USERNAME:
PASSWORD:
NOTES:

WEBSITE:
USERNAME:
PASSWORD:
NOTES:

Made in the USA
Monee, IL
24 July 2020